When Your
Parent Dies

When Your Parent Dies

written by
Daniel Fitzpatrick G.

illustrated by
R.W. Alley

ABBEY PRESS

Publications
St. Meinrad, IN 47577

Text © 2009 by Daniel Fitzpatrick G.
Illustrations © 2009 by Saint Meinrad Archabbey
Published by Abbey Press Publications
St. Meinrad, Indiana 47577

Library of Congress Catalog Number
2008940947

ISBN 978-0-87029-419-8

Printed in the United States of America.

Foreword

Adult children are expected to be "mature enough" to handle a parent's death. No matter your age, however, you never stop being your parent's child. And "the child within you" grieves their passing deeply.

At the same time, there is much you can hold onto at this time of loss. "A parent's love is never lost if passed on," wrote one author. Pass on that love to others—and treat yourself to the same loving care your parent gave to you. That love remains, and will endure forever.

Acknowledgement

The author wishes to acknowledge his debt to the wonderful ideas on this subject found in Abbey Press publications by Jim Auer, Carol Luebering, Peggy Heinzmann Ekerdt, Judy Ball, Linus Mundy, Lisa O. Engelhardt, Joel Schorn, Patrice Tuohy, Greg Long, and Steven Long. He dedicates this book to his dearly departed mother and to all who have grieved and grown from the loss of a parent.

1.

No matter how old you are, when a parent dies, a part of you feels orphaned. The world feels like a different place without your parent—smaller, colder, less friendly.

2.

When you are an adult, the death of your parent doesn't get a lot of recognition or support. Your loss may not be long remembered or widely acknowledged by others. You might feel pretty much alone in your grief.

3.

Though you might _feel_ alone, you _aren't_ alone. In fact, millions of adults grieve the loss of a parent every year. Many of them join support groups where they can talk to others who understand. You can, too.

4.

You may at times feel fear or even panic that catches you by surprise. But remember, you have lost the person who tucked you into bed at night and held your hand when you were scared as a child. It's natural to feel frightened at times.

5.

The death of a parent leaves us feeling abandoned, no matter how many loving people surround us. Parents aren't supposed to "leave us behind," but your parent left on a journey they must make without you. Their love remains, however, and can bring comfort.

6.

Don't wall off your grief. Find a way to cry and talk about your loss with someone who will understand. Find a trusted friend who will listen without judging, support without criticism, and simply be with you.

7.

Be gentle with yourself and others as you grieve. Give yourself time and space. Others can carry a bit of your load for a while at home and at work.

8.

You were not ready for this to happen. Even if you saw it coming, there is a sense of shock—after all, your "big, strong" parent has fallen. It's okay to feel that way.

9.

When your parent dies, you grieve many losses. You have lost a person whose love was absolute and unconditional, not like any other love on earth. Some have even compared it to God's love. This kind of love is hard to find, and harder to lose.

10.

Your parent was there for you as a child when you cried or hurt yourself. They stood up for you and watched out for you. It's natural that their death will touch that part of all of us that longs for comfort and protection.

11.

You may have lost a sense of your own identity. You have always been your parent's child; it's part of how you have defined yourself. Who are you now?

12.

It may be true, as someone
once said, that "You never really
grow up until your parent dies."
Now is your chance to rediscover
(or discover for the first time)
who you really are or want
to become.

13.

You've lost someone who was a key to your sense of family connection. Your parent helped keep the family tree rooted. Where do you go to "go home" for the holidays? How can you connect with them now?

For
Sale

14.

Your definition of "family" will have to undergo some changes. But that doesn't mean family members can't still be there for one another. It is now time for others—including you—to step forward to lead the way.

15.

Your best memories of time with your parent can be a source of healing, comfort, and hope. Gather with loved ones and share cherished memories. No one can take these from you.

16.

You may ponder what "might have been"—perhaps a vacation you planned to take with your parent "someday." It's okay to be aware of regrets, but avoid blaming yourself with "coulda, woulda, shoulda" thoughts. You did the best you could with the time you had.

17.

You can learn from your loss and turn your grief into growth. If your parent lived to be elderly, you have learned something about aging. Perhaps you can take a different view on your own priorities in life.

18.

When a parent dies, we lose our "Number One Fan." Your parent was there to say "Yes, you can" even when you weren't sure you could. You can still draw on that confidence.

19.

Amid the loss, recognize what remains. You will always have comforting memories. And think of the traits you inherited from your parent. Those will always be a part of who you are, too.

20.

You may feel a bit wounded inside, the result perhaps of not receiving all the nurturing you needed. You can take your wound to God in prayer; your eternal and loving Parent is able to heal all manner of hurt.

21.

Part of growing in wisdom is learning to heal the pain of the past. A counselor or religious leader can help you work through unresolved issues. Forgive your parent for having been "less than perfect."

22.

Remember that you are not the only one grieving. If you have kids, they have lost their grandparent, likely a very dear and tender person to them. Be extra mindful of their need to grieve, too.

23.

After a bit of time passes, maybe you can find ways to recognize what your parent has meant in the life of your family. Find a special place in your home for your parent's favorite rocking chair or lamp.

24.

Old sibling tensions may surface during caretaking, final arrangements, or over your parent's possessions. Realize that emotions run high and each of you grieves differently.

26.

Attend to present feelings. How are you feeling right now? Can you simply "be" with your emotions without trying to change them? Eventually they will pass, like clouds in the sky.

27.

You may have assumed that your parent would "always be there." But their passing is a part of life, like the passing of the seasons. Try to take comfort in the fact that all of life passes through the same cycles.

28.

Because grief can be intense, it's good to "put it aside" and "pick it up" again from time to time. Go to a funny movie or enjoy a good book so your mind is occupied with something other than your loss. Your parent would suggest as much!

29.

There is no need to feel guilty
for feeling good, for laughing
and enjoying life again. Your
parent would not want you to
suffer on their account. They
brought you into the world
to live a full life. Doing so is
the greatest honor you can
pay them.

30.

Prepare in advance for the "tough days"—holidays, birthdays, anniversaries, and milestones like graduations, marriage, or the birth of a child. You will feel your parent's absence more keenly at such times. Make a special effort to feel the connection that always will be there in your heart.

31.

As time passes and grief lingers, you may hear words like "I worry about you" or "You shouldn't feel so sad," or even "Isn't it time to move on with life?" But there is no reason either to push grief away or invite it to stay. It will follow its natural course, like a river to the sea. Your job simply is to navigate the waters!

32.

Find something tender and intimate of your parent's to keep close at hand—a favorite jacket, a ring, even a pair of slippers. Consider it a gift from your loved one that will help keep his or her memory alive for you in a way that brings a smile.

33.

Ask your parent's friends and associates to share a favorite memory with you at a memorial service or by letter or email. You can learn a great deal about your parent and collect the tributes in a memorial booklet to cherish over time.

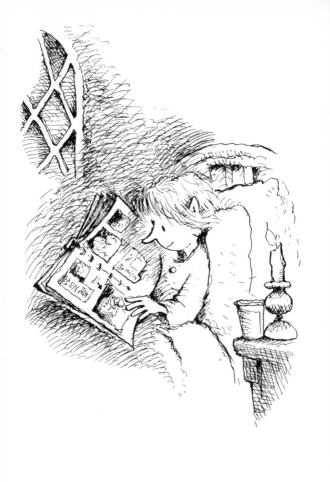

34.

You honor your parent's memory by putting their best qualities to work in your own life. If your parent was extra patient with you, you can strive for the same with others. If they modeled integrity and honesty, do the same in your own life. You are a living legacy to your parent.

35.

Find simple but special ways to preserve memories of your parent. Prepare their favorite meal every year on their birthday or hang an extra stocking on the mantle at the holidays. Find your own simple way to keep the connection alive.

36.

While it's true that a pillar of the family has passed, you can remain strong and united over time. Find new reasons and new places to gather on special days. A family reunion every summer is a great way to stay close.

37·

Your parent's passing invites you to address the "big questions" of life and to reexamine your faith. Use this opportunity to draw closer to God and a faith community.

38.

Belief in an eventual reunion in the afterlife is a great source of comfort. And your enduring love for your parent is all the proof you need that love is indeed stronger than death.

Daniel Fitzpatrick G. is a writer and editor, specializing in the areas of spirituality and personal healing.

Illustrator for the Abbey Press Elf-help Books, **R.W. Alley** also illustrates and writes children's books. He lives in Barrington, Rhode Island, with his wife, daughter, and son. See a wide variety of his works at: www.rwalley.com.

The Story of the Abbey Press Elves

The engaging figures that populate the Abbey Press "elf-help" line of publications and products first appeared in 1987 on the pages of a small self-help book called *Be-good-to-yourself Therapy*. Shaped by the publishing staff's vision and defined in R.W. Alley's inventive illustrations, they lived out the author's gentle, self-nurturing advice with charm, poignancy, and humor.

Reader response was so enthusiastic that more Elf-help Books were soon under way, a still-growing series that has inspired a line of related gift products.

The especially endearing character featured in the early books—sporting a cap with a mood-changing candle in its peak—has since been joined by a spirited female elf with flowers in her hair.

These two exuberant, sensitive, resourceful, kindhearted, lovable sprites, along with their lively elfin community, reveal what's truly important as they offer messages of joy and wonder, playfulness and co-creation, wholeness and serenity, the miracle of life and the mystery of God's love.

With wisdom and whimsy, these little creatures with long noses demonstrate the elf-help way to a rich and fulfilling life.

Elf-help Books

...adding "a little character" and a lot of help to self-help reading!

Available at your favorite gift shop or bookstore—
or directly from Abbey Press Publications,
St. Meinrad, IN 47577.
Call 1-800-325-2511.
www.abbeypresspublications.com